HEPTAMERON
OR
MAGICAL ELEMENTS
OF PETER DE ABANO

UNICURSAL

Copyright © 2024

Éditions Unicursal Publishers
unicursal.ca

ISBN 978-2-89806-605-4 (Paperback)
ISBN 978-2-89806-606-1 (Hardcover)

First English Edition, Imbolc 2024

HEPTAMERON

HEPTAMERON

OR

MAGICAL ELEMENTS

OF PETER DE ABANO

Philosopher, Disciple of Heinrich Cornelius

AGRIPPA.

In the former book, which is the fourth book of *Agrippa*, it is sufficiently spoken concerning Magical Ceremonies, and Initiations. But because he seemeth to have written to the learned, and well-experienced in this art; because he doth not specially treat of the Ceremonies, but rather speaketh of them in general, it was therefore thought good to adde hereunto the Magical Elements of *Peter de Abano*: that those who are hitherto ignorant, and have not tasted of Magical Superstitions, may have them in readiness, how they may exercise themselves therein.

For we see in this book, as it were a certain introduction of Magical vanity; and, as if they were in present exercise, they may behold the distinct functions of spirits, how they may be drawn to discourse and communication; what is to be done every day, and every hour; and how they shall be read, as if they were described sillable by sillable.

In brief, in this book are kept the principles of Magical conveyances. But because the greatest power is attributed to the Circles; (For they are certain fortresses to defend the operators safe from the evil Spirits;) In the first place we will treat concerning the composition of a Circle.

Of the Circle, & the Composition Thereof.

The form of Circles is not alwaies one and the same; but useth to be changed, according to the order of the Spirits that are to be called, their places, times, dayes and hours. For in making a Circle, it ought to be considered in what time of the year, what day, and what hour, that you make the Circle; what Spirits you would call, to what Star and Region they do belong, and what functions they have.

Therefore let there be made three Circles of the latitude of nine foot, and let them be distant one from another a hands breadth; and in the middle Circle, first, write:

1° The name of the hour wherein you do the work;

2° In the second place, Write the name of the Angel of the hour;

3° In the third place, The Sigil of the Angel of the hour;

4° Fourthly, The name of the Angel that ruleth that day wherein you do the work, and the names of his ministers;

5° In the fifth place, The name of the present time;

6° Sixthly, The name of the Spirits ruling in that part of time, and their Presidents;

7° Seventhly, The name of the head of the Signe ruling in that part of time wherein you work;

8° Eighthly, The name of the earth, according to that part of time wherein you work;

9° Ninthly, and for the compleating of the middle Circle, Write the name of the Sun and of the Moon, according to the said rule of time; for as the time is changed, so the names are to be altered.

And in the outermost Circle, let there be drawn in the four Angles, the names of the presidential Angels of the Air, that day wherein you would do this work; to wit, the name of the King and his three Ministers. Without the Circle, in four Angles, let *Pentagones* be made. In the inner Circle let there be written four divine names with crosses interposed in the middle of the Circle; to wit, towards the East let there be written *Alpha*, and towards the West let there be written *Omega;* and let a cross divide the middle of the Circle. When the Circle is thus finished, according to the rule now before written, you shall proceed.

Of the Names of the Hours, & the Angels ruling them.

It is also to be known, that the Angels do rule the hours in a successive order, according to the course of the heavens, and Planets unto which they are subject; so that that Spirit which governeth the day, ruleth also the first hour of the day; the second from this governeth the second hour; the third; the third hour, and so consequently.

And when seven Planets and hours have made their revolution, it returneth again to the first which ruleth the day. Therefore we shall first speak of the names of the hours:

Hours of the day.	*Hours of the night.*
1. Yayn.	13. Beron.
2. Janor.	14. Barol.
3. Nasnia.	15. Thami.
4. Salla.	16. Athir.
5. Sadedali.	17. Mathon.
6. Thamur.	18. Rana.
7. Ourer.	19. Netos.
8. Thamie.	20. Tafrac.
9. Neron.	21. Sassur.
10. Jayon.	22. Agla.
11. Abai.	23. Calerva.
12. Natalon.	24. Salam.

Of the names of the Angels and their Sigils, it shall be spoken in their proper places. Now let us take a view of the names of the times.

A year therefore is fourfold, and is divided into the Spring, Summer, Harvest and Winter; the names whereof are these:

The Spring . . . . . Talvi;
The Summer . Gasmaran;
Autumne . . . . Ardarael;
Winter . . . . Fallas.

The Angels of the Spring.
Caracasa, Coré, Amatiel, Commissoros.

Head of the signe: Spugliguel.
Name of the earth: Amadaï.
Name of the Sun: Abraym.
Name of the Moon: Agusita.

The Angels of the Summer.
Gargatel, Tariel, Gaviel.

Head of the signe: Tubiel.
Name of the earth: Festativi.
Name of the Sun: Athemay.
Name of the Moon: Armatas.

The Angels of Autumne.
Tarquam, Guabarel.

Head of the signe: Tarquaret.
Name of the earth: Rabianara.
Name of the Sun: Abragini.
Name of the Moon: Matasignais.

The Angels of Winter.
Amabael, Ctarari.

Head of the signe: Altarib.
Name of the earth: Gerenia.
Name of the Sun: Commutaf.
Name of the Moon: Affaterim.

THE CONSECRATIONS
& BENEDICTIONS.

Of the Benediction of the Circle.

When the Circle is ritely perfected, sprinkle the same with holy or purging water, and say:

Asperges me, Domine, hyssopo et mundabor: lavabia, et super nivem dealbabor.

The Benediction of Perfumes.

The perfumes which will be used for fumigations, say the following blessing, extending your hand over the perfumes:

God of Abraham, God of Isaac, God of Jacob, bless here the creatures of these kindes, that they may fill up the power and vertue of their odours; so that neither the enemy, nor any false imagination, may be able to enter into them: per Dominum nostrum Jesum-Christum, &c.

Then let them be sprinkled with holy water.

The Exorcisme of the fire upon which the Perfumes are to be put.

The fire which is to be used for suffumigations, is to be in a new vessel of earth or iron; and let it be exorcised after this manner, extending the hand:

I exorcise thee, O thou creature of fire, by him by whom all things are made, that forthwith thou cast away every phantasme from thee, that it shall not be able to do any hurt in anything. Then say, Bless, O Lord, this creature of fire, and sanctfie it, that it may be blessed to set forth the praise of thy holy name, that no hurt may come to the Exorcisers or Spectators: through our Lord Jesus Christ, &c.

Of the Garment and Pentacle.

L et it be a Priests Garment, if it can
be had, let it be of linen, and clean.
Then take this Pentacle made in the day
and hour of *Mercury*, the Moon increasing, written in parchment made of a Kids
skin. But first let there be said over it the
Mass of the holy Ghost, and let it be
sprinkled with water of baptism.

Oration to be said, when the
Vesture is put on.

A ncor, Amacor, Amides, Theodonias,
Anitor; by the merits of thy Angel, O
Lord, I will put on the Garments of Salvation,
that this which I desire I may bring to effect:
through thee the most holy Adonay, whose king-
dom endureth for ever and ever. Amen.

GREAT PENTACLE
OF SOLOMON.

Of the manner of working.

Let the Moon be increasing and equal, if it may then be done, and let her not be com bust. The Operator ought to be clean and purified by the space of nine dayes before the beginning of the work, and to be confessed, and receive the holy Communion. Let him have ready the perfume appropriated to the day wherein he would perform the work. He ought also to have holy water from a Priest, and a new earthen vessel with fire, a Vesture and a Pentacle; and let all these things be rightly and duly consecrated and prepared. Let one of the servants carry the earthen vessel full of fire, and the perfumes, and let another bear the Book, another the Garment and Pentacle, and let the master carry the Sword over which there must be said one mass of the Holy Ghost; and on the middle of the Sword, let there be written this name, *Agla* †, and on the other side thereof, this name † *On* †. And as he goeth to the consecrated place, let him continually read Letanies, the servants answering. And when he cometh to the place where he will erect the Circle, let him draw the lines of the Circle, as we have before taught: and after he hath made it, let him sprinkle the Circle with holy water, saying:

Asperges me, Domine, hyssopo et mundabor: lavabis me, et super nivem dealbabor.

The Master therefore ought to be purified with fasting, chastity, and abstinency from all luxury the space of three whole dayes before the day of the operation. And on the day that he would do the work, being clothed with pure garments, and furnished with Pentacles, Perfumes, and other things necessary hereunto, let him enter the Circle, and call the Angels from the four parts of the world, which do govern the seven Planets the seven dayes of the week, Colours and Metals; whose name you shall see in their places.

And with bended knees invocating the said Angels particularly, let him say:

O *Angeli supradicti, estote adjutores meæ pe-titioni, & in adjutorium mihi, in meis rebus & petitionibus.*

Translation.

O *Angels, be favorable to me and help me in my affairs and in my requests.*

Then let him call the Angels from the four parts of the world, that rule the Air the same day wherein he doth the work or experiment. And having implored special-ly all the Names and Spirits written in the Circle, let him say:

O *vos omnes, adjuro atque contestor per sedem Adonay, per Hagios, O Theos, Ischyros, Athanatos, Paracletos, Alpha & Omega, & per hæc tria nomina secreta, Agla, On, Tetragrammaton, quòd hodie debeatis adimplere quod cupio.*

Translation.

O all of you, I conjure you and call you to witness by the siege of Adonay, by Aghios, O Theos, Ischyros, Athanatos, Paracletus, Alpha & Omega, and by these three Secret Names: Agla, On, Tetragrammaton, that you must accomplish today what I ask.

These things being performed, let him read the Conjuration assigned for the day wherein he maketh the experiments, as we have before spoken; but if they shall be obstinate and refractory, and will not yield themselves obedient, neither to the Conjuration assigned to the day, nor to the prayers before made, then use the Conjurations and Exorcismes following.

Exorcisme of the Spirits of the Air.

Nos facti ad imaginem Dei, & ejus facti voluntate, per potentissimum & corroboratum nomen Dei El, forte & admirabile vos exorcizamus (here he shall name the Spirits he would have appear, of what order soever they be) & imperamus per eum qui dixit, & factum est, & per omnia nomina Dei, & per nomen Adonay, El, Elohim, Elohe, Zebaoth, Elion, Escerchie, Jah, Tetragrammaton, Sadai, Dominus Deus, excelsus, exorcizamus vos, atque potenter imperamus, ut appareatis statim nobis hic juxta Circulum in pulchra forma, videlicet humana, & sine deformitate & tortuositate aliqua. Venite vos omnes tales, quia vobis imperamus, per nomen Y & V quod Adam audivit, & locutus est: & per nomen Dei Agla, quod Loth audivit, & factus salvus cum sua familia: & per nomen Joth, quod Jacob audivit ab Angelo secum luctantes, & liberatus est de manu fratris sui Esau: & per nomen Anephexeton, quot Aaron audivit, & loquens, & sapiens factus est: & per nomen Zebaoth, quod Moses nominavit, & omnia flumina & paludes de terra Ægypti, versæ fuerunt in sanguinem: & per nomen Ecerchie Oriston, quod Moses nominavit, & omnes flu vis ebullierunt ranas, & ascenderunt in domos Ægyptiorum, omnia destruentes: & per nomen Elion, quod Moses nominavit, & fuit grando talis, qualis non fuit ab initio mundi:

*& per nomen Adonay, quod Moses nominavit,
& fuerunt locusta, & apparuerunt super terram
Ægyptiorum, & comederunt quæ residua erant
grandini: & per nomen Schemes amathia, quod
Joshua vocavit, & remoratus est Sol cursum: &
per nomen Alpha & Omega, quod Daniel nominavit, & destruxit Beel, & Draconem interfer-
it: & in nomine Emmanuel, quod tres pueri,
Sidrach, Misach & Abednago, in camino ignis
ardentis, cantaverunt, & liberati fuerunt: &
per nomen Hagios, & sedem Adonay, & per ò
Theos, Iscytos, Athanatos, Paracletus; & per hæc
tria secreta nomina, Agla, On, Tetragrammaton,
adjuro, contestor, & per hæc nomina, & per alia
nomina Domini nostri Dei Omnipotentis, vivi
& veri, vos qui vestra culpa de Coelis ejecti fuistis
usque ad infernum locum, exorcizamus, & viriliter imperamus, per eum qui dixit, & factum est,
cui omnes obediunt creaturæ, & per illud tremen-
dum Dei judicium: & per mare omnibus incer-
tum, vitreum, quod est amte conspectum divinæ
majestatis gradiens, & potestiale: & per quatuor
divina animalia T. antè sedem divinæ majesta is
gradientia, & oculos antè & retrò habentia: &
per ignem ante ejus thronum circumstantem: &*

per sanctos Angelos Cælorum, T. & per eam quæ Ecclesia Dei nominatur: & per summam sapientiam Omnipotentis Dei viriliter exorcizamus, ut nobis hic ante Circulum appareatis, ut faciendam nostram voluntatem, in omnibus prout placuerit nobis: per sedem Baldachiæ, & per hoc nomen Primeumaton, quod Moses nominavit, & in cavernis abyssi fuerunt profundati vel absorpti, Datan, Corah & Abiron: & in virtute istius nominis Primeumaton, tota Coeli militia compellente, maledicimus vos, privamus vos omni officio, loco & gaudio vestro, esque in profundum abyssi, & usque ad ultimum diem judicii vos ponimus, & relegamus in ignem æternum, & in stagnum ignis & sulphuris, nisi statim appareatis hic coram nobis, inte Circulum, ad faciendum voluntatem nostram. In omnibus venite per hæc nomina, Adonay Zebaoth, Adonay, Amioram. Venite, venite, imperat vobis Adonay, Saday, Rex regum potentissimus & tremendissimus, cujus vires nulla subterfugere potest creatura vobis pertinacissimis futuris nisi obedieritis, & appareatis ante hunc Circulum, affabiles subito, tandem ruina flebilis miserabilisque, & ignis perpetuum inextinguibilis vos manet. Venite ergo in nom-

ine Adonay Zebaoth, Adonay Amioram: venite, venite, quid tardatis? festinate imperat vobis Adonay, Saday, Rex regum, El Aty, Titeip, Azia, Hyn, Jen, Minosel, Achadan, Uay, Vaa, Ey, Haa, Eye, Exe, à El, El, El, à Hy, Hau, Hau, Hau, Va, Va, Va, Va.

Translation.

*W*e, made in the image of God, endowed with the power of God, and made by His will, we exorcise you (here he will name the spirits he wishes, of whatever orders they may be) by the Almighty, most established, strong and admirable name of God, EL, and command you by Him who said, and all was done; and by all the names of God: Adonay, El, Elohim, Zebaoth, Elion, Escerchie, Iah, Tetragrammaton, Saday, the Lord God, Most High: we exorcise you and forcefully command you to appear at once around this Circle, in a beautiful form, that is, human, and without any deformity or blemish. Come all thus, because we command you, by the name Y and V, which Adam heard and spoke; and by the name of God, Agla, which Lot heard and

which made him and his family safe, and by the
name Iod which Jacob heard from the Angel with
whom he wrestled and by which he was delivered
from the hand of his brother Esau ; and by the
name Anephexeton, which Aaron heard, and
which made him speak and wise; and by the name
Zebaoth, which Moses uttered, and turned all the
rivers and marshes of Egypt into blood; and by
the name Escerchie Oriston, which Moses named,
and brought out of the rivers the frogs that invad-
ed the houses of the Egyptians ; and by the name
Elion, which Moses pronounced, and caused such
a great hail to fall that no such hail has been seen
since the beginning of the world; and by the name
Adonay, which Moses named, and produced that
prodigious quantity of locusts that appeared in
Egypt and ate what had not been destroyed by the
hail; and by the name Schèmes Amathia, which
Joshua named, and stopped the course of the
Sun, and by the name Alpha and Omega, which
Daniel named, by which he destroyed Bel and
killed the Dragon; and by the name Emmanuel,
which the three children: Sidrach, Misach and
Abdenago sang in the fiery furnace, and by
which they were delivered; and by Aghios, and by

the Seat of Adonay, and by O Theos Ischiros, Athanatos, Paracletus; and by these three Secret Names: Agla, On, Tetragrammaton, I conjure you and take you to witness, and by all these names, and by all the names of our Lord, God almighty, true and living; you who by your sin have been cast out of Heaven and cast into Hell, we strongly exorcise and command you by Him who having said, and all was done, to whom all creatures obey ; and by this terrible judgment of God which is to be feared; and by the sea which is an element on which no one can count anything certain, transparent as glass, which is in the presence of the divine Majesty, ready to ascend according to the power God will give it; and by the four divine animals T. which are on the degrees of the seat of the divine Majesty, and which have eyes before and behind; and by the Fire which surrounds his Throne; and because which is called the Church of God; and by the supreme wisdom of Almighty God ; we strongly exorcise you to appear before this Circle, to do our will in whatever we please, by the seat of Balmachia and by that name Primeumaton, which Moses named and precipitated Datan, Corel and Abiron into *the depths of the abysses; and by virtue of that same name Primeumaton, which makes all the heavenly, earthly Militia, and the Underworld tremble; we curse you, we deprive you of all offices and functions, and of all pleasures you may have, we place and relegate you to eternal fire and to the lake of fire and brimstone ; into the depths of the Abyss, and until the last day of judgment, if you do not appear to us at once, before this Circle, to do our will in all things; come by these names Adonay, Zebaoth, Adonay, come, come, Adonay commands you, this most powerful and most to be feared King of kings, whose strength and power no creature can evade. If you persist in your extreme obstinacy, and if before this Circle you do not appear to us at once, gentle and affable, you can expect only a lamentable and miserable ruin, and a fire that can never be extinguished. Come then in the name of Adonay Zebaoth, Adonay, Amioram. Come, come, why do you delay? Hurry at once! This is commanded you by Adonay Saday, the King of kings, El Aty, Titeip, Azia, Hyn, Jen, Minosel, Achadan, Uay, Vaa, Ey, Haa, Eye, Exe, à El, El, El, à Hy, Hau, Hau, Hau, Va, Va, Va, Va.*

ORISON TO GOD
To be said in the four parts
of the World, in the Circle.

Amorule, Tancha, Latisten, Rabur, Escha, Aladia, Alpha & Omega, Leyste, Oriston, Adonay: O my most merciful heavenly Father, have mercy upon me, although a sinner; make appear the arm of thy power in me this day (although thy unworthy child) against these obstinate and pernicious Spirits, that I by thy will may be made a contemplator of thy divine works, and may be illustrated with all wisdom, and alwaies worship and glorifie thy name. I humbly implore and beseech thee, that these Spirits which I call by thy judgement, may be bound and constrained to come, and give true and perfect answers to those things which I shall ask them, and that they may declare and shew unto us those things which by me or us shall be commanded them, not hurting any creature, neither injuring nor terrifying me or my fellows, nor hurting any other creature, and affrighting no man; but let them be obedient to my requests, in all these things which I command them.

Then let him stand in the middle of the Circle, and hold his hand towards the Pentacle, and say:

Per Pentaculum Salomonis advocavi, dent mihi responsum verum.

Translation.

I call you by the virtue of the Pentacle of Solomon; give me a true answer.

Let him wait a moment, then let him say:

Beralanensis, Baldachiensis, Paumachiæ & Apologiæ sedes, per Reges potestaiesiá magnanimas, ac principes præpotentes, genio Liachidæ, ministri tartareæ sedes: Primac, hic princeps sedis Apologiæ nona cohorte: Ego vos invoco, & invocando vos conjure, atque supernæ Majestatis munitus virtute, potenter impero, per eum qui dixit, & factum est, & cui obediunt omnes creaturæ: & per hoc nomen ineffabile, Tetragrammaton יהוה Jehovah, in quo est plasmatum omne seculum, quo audito elementa

corruunt, aer concutitur, mare retrograditur, ig-
nis extinguitur, tera tremit, omnesque exercitus
Coelestium, Terrestrium, & Infernorum tre-
munt, turbantur & corruunt: quatenus citò &
sine mora & omni occasione remota, ab univer-
sis mundi partibus veniatis, & rationabiliter de
omnibus quæcunque interrogavero, respondeatis
vos, & veniatis pacifice, visibiles, & affabiles:
nunc & sine mora manifestantes quod cupimus:
conjurati per nomen æterni vivi & veri Dei
Helioren, & mandata nostra per ficientes, per-
sistentes semper usque ad finem, & intentionem
meam, visibiles nobis, & affabiles, clara voce no-
bis, intelligibile, & sine omni ambiguitate.

Translation.

Seat of Beretaneuse, Baldachia, Paumachia
and Apologia, I invoke you by the Kings, and
the magnanimous Powers, and the very powerful
Princes, by the spirit of Liachidae, minister of
Tartarus; Primac, who are here the Prince of the
Seat of Apologia in the ninth cohort, I conjure
you, and equipped with the virtue of the Supreme
Majesty, I command you powerfully by Him
who having said, and all was done, and to whom

all creatures obey, and by this ineffable name, Tetragrammaton, Jehovah, who is the source and origin of all centuries, in whose name the elements merge, the air is struck and shaken, the sea goes against its common course, the fire goes out, the earth trembles, all the celestial, terrestrial and infernal armies tremble, are disturbed and are in a violent movement of ruin, this is why at the moment and without any pretext of delay for any occasion whatever, come from all parts of the world, and answer me properly on everything I ask you. Come now and without any delay, as we wish, conjured as you are by the name of God Helioren, eternal, living and true; and do what we command you, always persisting in our intentions until the end; appear before us, visible, gentle and affable, answering us with a clear and intelligible voice, and without any ambiguity.

Visions and Apparitions.

These things being done exactly, there will appear an infinity of visions and phantoms playing all kinds of musical instruments; the Spirits do this to frighten the Disciples and force them to leave the Circle, because they can do nothing against the one who carries out the operation; then you will see an infinity of people armed with arrows, with a multitude of horrible beasts standing ready to devour the Disciples who, however, have nothing to fear. Then, the Priest or Exorcist, extending his hand over the Pentacle, must say:

Fugiat hinc iniquitas vestra, vittute vexilli Dei.

Translation.
May your prestige cease by the virtue of the crucified God.

Then, the Spirits will be forced to obey the Exorcist, and the Disciples will be at peace and will no longer see horrible forms. Then let the Exorcist say, stretching out his hand to the Pentacle:

Ecce Pentaculum Salomonis, quod ante vestram adduxi præsentiam: ecce personam exorcizatoris on medio Exorcismi, qui est optimà à Deo munitus, intrepidus, providus, qui viribus potens vos exorcizando invocavit & vocat. Venite ergo cum festinotione in virtute nominum istorum, Aye, Saraye, Aye, Saraye, Aye Saraye, ne differatis venire, per nomina æterna Dei vivi & veri Eloy, Archima, Rabur: & per hoc præsens Pentaculum, quod super vos potenter imperat: & per virutem coelestium Spirituum dominorum vestrorum: & per personam exorcizatoris, conjurati, festinati venire & obedire præceptori vestro, qui vocatur Octinomos.

Translation.

Behold the Pentacle of Solomon that I present to you. Here is also the person of the Master in the middle of the exorcism, who is very well equipped by the power of God, fearless and provided with everything, who being very powerful in strength, has invoked you by exorcising you, and calls you. Come then, and haste, by virtue of these names: Age, Saraye, Aye, Saraye, do not delay coming by the eternal names of the liv-

*ing and true God, Eloy, Circhina, Rabur; and
by this Pentacle which powerfully commands over
you, and by the virtue of the celestial Spirits, your
Masters, and by the person of the Exorcist, conjured as you are, haste, and obey your Master who
is called Octinomos.*

This being done, blow into the four
corners of the world, and you will immediately see great movements. Then say:

*Quid tardatis? Quid moramini? Quid fac-
tis? Præparate vos & obedite præceptori vesto, in
nomine Domini Bathat, vel Vachat super Abrac
ruens, super veniens, Abeor super Aberer.*

Translation.
*Why are you delaying? What are you doing?
Prepare to obey your Master promptly, in the
name of Lord Bathat or Vachat rushing towards
Abrac, occurring Abeor on Aberer.*

Then they will come immediately in
their own forms, and when you see them
near the Circle, show them the Pentacle

covered with a Holy Shroud, uncover it for then, and say:

Ecce conclusionem vestram, nolite fieri inobedientes.

Translation.
This is your last term; do not be disobedient.

Immediately, you will see them in a peaceful form, and they will say: *Ask what you want, we are ready to obey your commandments, because the Lord has submitted to us.*

And when they have appeared thus, say to them:

Bene veneritis Spiritus, vel reges nobilissimi, quia vos vocavi per illum cui omne genuflectitur, coelestium, terrestrium & infernorum: cujus in manu omnia regna regum sunt, nec est qui suæ contrarius esse possit Majestati. Quatenus constringo vos, ut hic ante circulum visibes, affabiles permanetis, tamdiu tamque constantes, nec sint licentia mea recedatis, donec meam sine fallacia

aliqua & veredicè perficiatis voluntatem, per po-
tentiæ illius virtutem, qui mare posuit terminum
suum, quem præterire non potest, & lege illius
potentiæ, non periransit fines suos, Dei scilicet al-
tissimi, regis, domini, qui cuncta creavit, Amen.

Translation.

Welcome, most noble Spirits or Kings, be-
cause I have called you by Him in whose name
every knee must bent, of the celestial, terrestrial
and infernal; in whose hand are the kingdoms
of all kings, and to whose majesty no one can be
contrary; this is why I force you to remain before
this Circle, visible and affable, without you being
able to leave before my saying, and until you have
accomplished my will, exactly and without any de-
ception, by the virtue and power of Him who gave
to the sea limits which it cannot pass and which it
cannot overflow by the law of this power, namely
the Most High God, King, Lord, who created all
things. Amen.

Then command what you will, and it
shall be done. Afterwards license them
thus:

† In nomine Patris, † Filii, & † Spiritus sancti, ite in pace ad loca vestra: & pax sit inter nos & vos, parati sitis venire vocati.

Translation.

In the name of the Father †, and of the Son †, and of the Hole Spirit †: go in peace to your abodes, and may peace be between you and us; and always be ready to come when you will be called.

These are the things which *Peter de Abano* hath spoken concerning Magical Elements. But that you may the better know the manner of composing a Circle, I will set down one Scheme; so that if any one would make a Circle in Spring-time for the first hour of Lords day, it must be in the same manner as is the figure following. It remaineth now, that we explain the week, the several dayes thereof : and first of the Lords day.

The figure of a Circle for the first
hour of the Lords day, in Spring-time

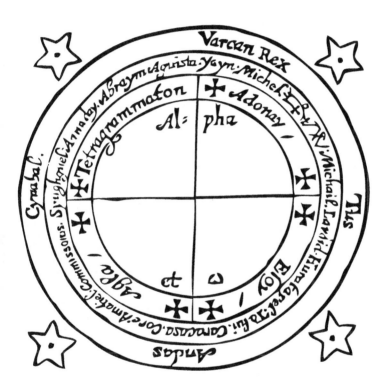

CONSIDERATIONS
& CONJURATIONS
FOR THE SEVEN
DAYS OF THE WEEK.

CONSIDERATIONS OF THE LORDS DAY.

The Angel of the Lords day, his Sigil, Planet, the Signe of the Planet, and the name of the fourth heaven:

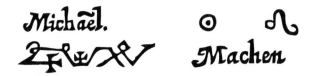

The Angels of the Lords day:
Michael, Dardiel, Huratapel.

The Angels of the air ruling on the Lords day: Varcan, king. Tus, Andras, Cynabal, ministers.

The winde which the Angels of the air abovesaid are under: Boreas (The North-winde.)

The Angel of the fourth heaven, ruling on the Lords day, which ought to be called from the four parts of the world:

At the east: Samael, Gabriel, Baciel, Vionatrabar, Atel.

At the west: Anael, Burchat, Pabel, Suceratos, Vestael, Capabili.

At the north: Aiel, Saphiel, Aniel, vel Aquiel, Matuyel, Masgabriel.

At the south: Habudiel, Uriel, Machasiel, Naromiel, Charsiel.

The perfume of the Lords day: Red Sandalwood.

The Conjuration of the Lords day.

Conjuro & confirmo super vos Angeli fortes Dei, & sancti, in nomine Adonay, Eye, Eye, Eye, qui est ille, qui fuit, est & erit, Eye, Abraye: & in nomine Saday, Cados, Cados, Cados, alie sendentis super Cherubin, & per nomen magnum ipsius Dei fortis & potentis, exaltatique super omnes coelos, Eye, Saraye, plasmatoris seculorum, qui creavit mundum, coelum, terram, mare, & omnia quæ in eis sunt in primo die, & sigillavit ea sancto nomine suo Phaa: & per nomina sanctorum Angelorum, qui domin-

antur in quarto exercitu, & serviunt coram po-
tentissimo Salamia, Angelo magno & honorato:
& per nomen stellæ, quæ est Sol, & per signum,
& per immensum nomen Dei vivi, & per nom-
ina omnia prædicta, conjuro te Michael angele
magne, qui es præpositus Diei Dominicæ: & per
nomen Adona, Dei Israel, qui creavit mundum
& quicquid in eo est, quod pro melabores, &
ad moleas omnem meam petitionem, juxta meum
velle & votum meum, in negotio & causa mea.

Translation.

I conjure you and confirm over you; Angels of
God, very strong and very holy, in the name
of Adonay, Eye, Eye, Eye, who is He who was,
is and will be, Eye, Abiaye, and in the name
of Saday, Cados, Cados, Cados, who sits high
above the Cherubim, and by the great name of
this strong and powerful God, and who is exalted
above all the Heavens, Eye, Saray, the Maker of
the ages, who first created the world , the sky, the
earth, the sea, and all things that are therein, and
who has sealed them with his holy name Phaa,
and by the names of the holy Angels who rule
in the fourth army, and who serve in the presence
of the most powerful Salamia, great and honored
Angel; and by the name of the star which is the

Sun, and by the sign and by the immense name of the living God, and by all the names mentioned above, I conjure you Michael, great Angel, who is appointed for Sunday, and by the name of Adonay, God of Israel, who created the world and all that is within, to work for me and to fulfill all my request according to my will and desire, in my work and my cause.

And here thou shalt declare thy cause and business, and for what thing thou makest this Conjuration; for example, if it is about money, you will say:

Bring me here this instant one hundred Louis d'or, coined, valid & profitable, for whatever we want to use them for.

The Spirits of the air of the Lords day, are under the North-winde; their nature is to procure Gold, Gemmes, Carbuncles, Riches; to cause one to obtain favour and benevolence; to dissolve the enmities of men; to raise men to honors; to carry or take away infirmities. But in what manner they appear, it's spoken already in the former book of Magical Ceremonies.

Common Forms of the Spirits of the Sun on the Lords day.

They most often appear with a large and elongated body, bloody and coarse, of a golden color with a tincture of blood; their movement is the radiance and brilliance of the sky, and their sign is to excite sweat in him who conjures them and compels them to come to him.

Their particular forms are:

A king, a scepter in hand, mounted on a lion;

A king, crowned;

A queen, holding a scepter in hand;

A bird;

A lion;

A rooster;

A garment of saffron or gold color.

A scepter.

A man with a tail.

CONSIDERATIONS OF MONDAY.

The Angel of Monday, his Sigil, Planet, the Signe of the Planet, and name of the first heaven:

The Angels of Monday: Gabriel, Michael, Samael.

The Angels of the air ruling on Monday: Arcan, king. Bile, Missabu, Abuzalia, ministers.

The winde which the said Angels of the air are subject to: Zephyrus (The West-winde).

The Angels of the first heaven, ruling on Monday, which ought to be called from the four parts of the world:

At the east: Gabriel, Deamiel, Gabrael, Janael, Madiel.

At the west: Sachiel, Bachanael, Zaniel, Corabiet, Habaiel.

At the north: Mael, Baliel, Vael, Balay, Valnum, Humastrau.

At the south: Curaniel, Lanun, Dabriel, Anayl, Darquiel, Vetuel.

The perfume of Monday: Aloes.

The Conjuration of Monday.

Conjuro & confirmo super vos Angeli fortes & boni, in nomine Adonay, Adonay, Adonay, Eie, Eie, Eie, Cados, Cados, Cados, Achim, Achim, Ja, Ja, Fortis, Ja, qui apparuis monte Sinai, cum glorificatione regis Adonay, Saday, Zebaoth, Anathay, Ya, Ya, Ya, Marinata, Abim, Jeia, qui maria creavit stagna & omnes aquas in secundo die, quasdam super coelos, & quosdam in terra. Sigillavit mare in alio nomine suo, & terminum, quam sibi posuit, non præteribit: & per nomina Angelorum, qui dominantur in primo exercitu, qui serviunt

*Orphaniel Angelo magno, precioso & honorato :
& per nomen Stellæ, quæ est Lunæ : & per nomina prædicta, super te conjuro, scilicet Gabriel,
qui es præpositus diei. Lunæ secundo quòd pro
me labores & adimpleas, &c.*

Translation.

*I conjure you and confirm over you, strong and
good Angels, in the name of Adonay, Adonay,
Adonay, Eiè, Eiè, Eiè, Cados. Cados, Cados,
Achim, Achim, Achim, Ja, Ja, of strong Ja, who
appeared at Mount Sinai, with the glorification of
king Adonay, Saday, Zebaoth, Amathoy, Ya, Ya,
Ya, Marinata Abim, Jeia, who created on the second
day the seas and the ponds and all the waters, both
in the earth and on the earth. He has sealed the
sea with his name Most High, and it will not pass
the bounds that he has given it, and by the names
of the Angels who rule in the first army, who serve
Orphaniel, great, precious and honored Angel; and
by the name of the star which is the Moon, and by
the above mentioned names, I conjure you, Gabriel,
who is in charge of Monday which is the second
day, to work for me and accomplish, etc... (Here,
like on Sunday, we specify what we want).*

The Spirits of the air of Monday, are subject to the West-winde, which is the winde of the Moon: their nature is to give silver; to convey things from place to place; to make horses swift, and to disclose the secrets of persons both present and future: but in what manner they appear, you may see in the former book.

Common Forms of the Spirits of the Moon on Monday.

Their bodies are usually large, phlegmatic, their color like that of a dark and tenebrous cloud, their faces swollen, their eyes red and full of water, their heads bald, their teeth like wild boars. Their movements are similar to those of a great storm at sea. The sign which will manifest their approach to the Circle will be an abundant rain.

Their particular forms are:

A king armed with a bow, with arrows, and mounted on a deer;

A small child;

A huntress armed with a bow and arrows;

A cow;

A little deer;

A goose;

A green or silver colored outfit;

An arrow;

A multi-footed animal.

CONSIDERATIONS OF TUESDAY.

The Angel of Tuesday, his sigil, his Planet, the Signe governing that Planet, and the name of the fifth heaven:

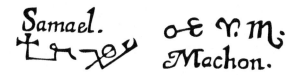

The Angels of Tuesday: Samael, Satael, Amabiel.

The Angels of the air ruling on Tuesday: Samax, king. Carmax, Ismoli, Paffran, ministers.

The winde to which the said Angels are subject: Subsolanus (The East-winde).

The Angels of the fifth heaven ruling on Tuesday, which ought to be called from the four parts of the world:

At the east: Friagne, Glizas, Guael, Arragon, Damael.

At the west: Lama, Soncas, Irel, Astagna, Iaxel, Lobquin, Isiael.

At the north: Rahumel, Seraphiel, Hyniel, Mathiel, Rayel, Fraciel.

At the south: Sacriet, Osael, Ianiel, Vianuel, Galdel, Zaliel.

The perfume of Tuesday: Pepper.

The Conjuration of Tuesday.

Conjuro & confirmo super vos, Angeli fortes & sancti, per nomen Ya, Ya, Ya, He, He, He, Va, Hy, Hy, Ha, Ha, Ha, Va, Va, Va, An, An, An, Aie, Aie, Aie, El, Ay, Elibra, Eloim, Eloim: & per nomina ipsius alti Dei, qui secit aquam aridam apparere, & vocavit terram, & produxit arbores, & herbas de ea, & sigillavit super eam cum precioso, honorato, metuendo & sancto nomine suo: & per nomen angelorum dominantium in quinto exercitu, qui serviunt Acimoy Angelo magno, forti, potenti, & honorato: & per nomen Stellæ, quæ est Mars: & per nomina prædicta conjuro super te Samael, Angele magne, qui præpositus es diei Martis: &

per nomina Adonay, Dei vivi & veri, quod pro
me labores, & adimpleas, &c.

Translation.

I conjure and confirm over you, strong and holy
Angels, by the name Ya, Ya, Ya, He, He,
He, Va, Hy, Hy, Ha, Ha, Ha, Va, Va, Va,
An, An, An, Aie, Aie, Aie, El, Ay, Elibra,
Eloim, Eloim: and by the names of this Most
High God, who made the water dry and called
it earth, who produced trees and herbs on its sur-
face, and who sealed it with his holy, precious and
adorable Name; and by the name of the Angels
who rule in the fifth army, who serve Acimoy,
great, strong, powerful and honored Angel; and
by the name of the star which is Mars; and by the
above mentioned names, I conjure you, Samael,
great Angel who is in charge of Tuesday, and by
the names of Adonay, living and true God, that
you work for me and accomplish, etc... (as in the
conjuration of Sunday).

The Spirits of the air of Tuesday are
under the East-winde: their nature is to
cause wars, mortality, death and combus-

tions; and to give ten thousand Soldiers
at a time; to bring death, infirmities or
health. The manner of their appearing
you may see in the former book.

Common Forms of the Spirits of Mars on Tuesday.

They will appear for a long time with
a bilious and very ugly face, of a slightly
brown color, turning to red, having horns
similar to those of a deer and the claws
of a griffin. They bellow like raging bulls;
their movement is like of a lit fire; and the
sign that they are approaching the Circle
is lightning and thunder.

Their particular forms are:
An armed king mounted on a wolf;
A red coat;
An armed man;
A woman holding a shield on her thigh;
A goat;
A horse;

A deer;
Sheep's wool or fleece;
A man with many heads.

CONSIDERATIONS OF WEDNESDAY

The Angel of Wednesday, his Sigil, Planet, the Signe governing that Planet, and the name of the second heaven:

The Angels of Wednesday: Raphael, Miel, Seraphiel.

The Angels of the air ruling on Wednesday: Modiat, or Modiat, king. Suquinos, Sallales, ministers.

The winde to which the said Angels of the air are subject: Africus (The Southwest-winde).

The Angels of the second heaven govern Wednesday, which ought to be called from the four parts of the world:

At the east: Mathlaï, Tarmiel, Baraborat.

At the west: Jerescue, Mitraton.

At the north: Thiel, Venahel, Veirnuel, Rael, Vetel, Jariachel, Abuiori.

At the south: Mittiel, Caluel, Netapa, Vel, Babel, Laquel.

The perfume of Wednesday: Mastic.

The Conjuration of Wednesday.

*C*onjuro *&* confirmo vos angeli fortes, sancti *& potentes, in nomine fortis, metuendissimi & benedicti Ja, Adonay, Eloim, Saday, Saday, Saday, Eie, Eie, Eie, Asamie, Asaraie: & in nomine Adonay Dei Israel, qui creavit luminaria magna, ad distinguendum diem à nocte: & per nomen omnium Angelorum deservientium in exercitu secundo coram Tetra Angelo majori, atque forti & potenti: & per nomen Stellæ, quæ est Mercurius: & per nomen Sigilli, quæ sigillatur a Deo fortissimo & honoratio: per omnia prædicta super te Raphael Angele magne, conjuro, qui es præpositus die: quartæ: & per nom-*

en sanctum quod erat scriptum in fronte Aaron sacerdotis altissimi creatoris: & per nomina Angelorum qui in gratiam Salvatoris confirmati sunt: & per nomen sedis Animalium, habentium senas alas, quòd pro me labores, &c.

Translation.

I conjure you and confirm over you, strong and powerful Angels, in the name of the strong, most formidable and blessed Ja, Adonay, Elohim, Saday, Saday, Saday, Eye, Eye, Eye, As Amie, Asaray; and in the name of Adonay, God of Israel, who created the great lights to distinguish day from night; and by the name of all the Angels who serve in the second army, in the presence of Tetra, the major Angel, strong and powerful, and by the name of the star which is Mercury, and by the name of the seal with which God, very strong and honored sealed it; by all the above mentioned things, I conjure you, Raphael, great Angel who is in charge of Wednesday which is the fourth day; and by the holy name which was written on the forehead of Aaron, the very high Priest of the Creator; and by the name of the Angels who are confirmed in the grace of the Savior; and by *the name of the throne of the animals which have healthy wings, that you work for me, etc... (as in the Sunday conjuration).*

The Spirits of the air of Wednesday are subject to the South-west-winde: their nature is to give all Metals; to reveal all earthly things past, present and to come; to pacific judges, to give victories in war, to re-edifie, and teach experiments and all decayed Sciences, and to change bodies mixt of Elements conditionally out of one into another; to give infirmities or health; to raise the poor, and cast down the high ones; to binde or lose Spirits; to open locks or bolts: such-kinde of Spirits have the operation of others, but not in their perfect power, but in virtue or knowledge. The what manner they appear, it is before spoken.

Common Forms of the Spirits of Mercury on Wednesday.

They will most often appear with a body of average size, cold, damp, beautiful; of an affable conversation, of a human face like an armed man, of a brilliant and dazzling color; their movement is similar to that of a clear cloud; their sign is to cause great fear to the one who conjures them and makes them come to him.

Their particular forms are:
A king riding on a bear;
A handsome young man;
A woman holding a cattail;
A dog;
A bear;
A magpie;
A multi-colored outfit;
A rod;
A stick.

CONSIDERATIONS OF THURSDAY.

The Angel of Thursday, his Sigil, Planet, the Signe of the Planet, and the name of the sixth heaven:

Sachiel. ♃ ⊕ ♓
Zebul.

The Angels of Thursday: Sachiel, Castiel, Asasiel.

The Angels of the air governing Thursday: Guth, king. Maguth, Gutriz, ministers.

The winde which the said Angels of the air are under: Notus (The South-winde).

But because there are no Angels of the air to be found above the fifth heaven, therefore on Thursday say the following prayers in the four parts of the world:

At the east:

O Deus magne & excelse, & honorate, per infinita secula.

O God, great and most high, and honored by all the infinite centuries.

At the west:

O Deus sapiens, & clare, & juste, ac divina clementia: ego rogo te piissime Pater, quòd meam petitionem, quòd meum opus, & meum laborem hodie debeam complere, & perfeclè intelligere. Tu qui vivis & regnas per infinita secula seculorum, Amen.

O wise, illustrious and fair God, and of divine clemency, I pray to you, my most pious Father, that I may today accomplish my request, my operation and my work, and make them perfectly: you who live and reign throughout all the infinite centuries of centuries. Amen.

At the north:

O Deus potens, fortis, & sine principio.

O God mighty, strong and without any beginning.

At the south:

O Deus potens & Misericors.

O mighty and merciful God.

The perfume of Thursday: Saffron.

The Conjuration of Thursday.

Conjuro & confirmo super vos, Angeli sancti, per nomen, Cados, Cados, Cados, Eschereie, Eschereie, Eschereie, Hatim ya, fortis firmator seculorum, Cantine, Jaym, Janic, Anic, Calbat, Sabbac, Berifay, Alnaym: & per nomen Adonay, qui creavit pisces reptilia in aquis, & aves super faciem terræ, volantes versus coelos die quinto: & per nomina Angelorum serventium in sexto exercitu coram pastore Angelo sancto & magno & potenti principe: & per nomen stellæ, quæ est Jupiter: & per nomen Sigilli sui: & per nomen Adonay, summi Dei, omnium creatoris: & per nomen omnium stellarum, & per vim & virtutem earum: & per nomina prædicta, conjuro te Sachiel Angele magne, qui es præpositus dici Jovis, ut pro me labores, &c.

Translation.

I conjure and confirm over you, Holy Angels, by the name Cados, Cados, Cados, Eschercie, Eschercie, Eschercie, Hatim Ya, strong support of the centuries, Cantin, Jaym, Janic, Anie, Calbat, Sabbac, Berifay, Alnaym; and by the name Adonay, who on the fifth day created fish and reptiles in the waters, and birds on the earth flying to the Heavens; and by the names of the Angels who serve in the sixth army, in the presence of the Shepherd Angel, holy, great and powerful prince; and by the name of the star which is Jupiter; and by the name of his seal; and by the name of Adonay, sovereign God creator of all things; and by the name of all the stars, and by their strength and virtue, and by the names aforesaid, I conjure you, Sachiel, great Angel, who is appointed to Thursday, to work for me, and to accomplish, etc... (as on Sunday).

The Spirits of the air of Thursday, are subject to the South-winde; their nature is to procure the love of woman; to cause men to be merry and joyful; to pacifie strife and contentions; to appease ene-

mies; to heal the diseased, and to disease
the whole; and procureth losses, or taketh
them away. Their manner of appearing is
spoken of already.

Common Forms of the Spirits of Jupiter on Thursday.

They appear with a sanguine and bilious body, of average size, in a horrible
and terrible movement; with a very gentle
look, a pleasant conversation, of an iron
color. Their movement is a flash accom-
panied by the sound of thunder, and the
sign that they will approach the Circle will
be that it will seem to you as if being de-
voured by lions.

Their particular forms are:

A king, with a drawn sword in hand,
on a deer;

A man dressed very long and wearing
a mitre;

A young girl adorned with flowers and crowned with laurel;

A bull;

A deer;

A peacock;

An azure-colored outfit;

A sword;

A flute.

CONSIDERATIONS OF FRIDAY.

The Angel of Friday, his Sigil, his Planet, the Signe governing that Planet, and name of the third heaven:

The Angels of Friday: Anael, Rachiel, Sachiel.

The Angels of the air reigning on Friday: Sarabotes, king. Amabiel Aba, Abalitoth Flaef, ministers.

The winde which the said Angels of the air are under: Zephyrus (The West-winde).

Angels of the third heaven, ruling on Friday, which are to be called from the four parts of the world:

At the east: Setchiel, Tamael, Chedusitaniel, Tenaciel, Corat.

At the west: Turiel, Kadie, Coniel, Maltiel, Babiel, Huphaltiel.

At the north: Peniel, Raphael, Penael, Raniel, Penat, Doremiel.

At the south: Porna, Samael, Sachiel, Santanael, Chermiel, Faniel.

The perfume of Friday: Pepperwort.

The Conjuration of Friday.

Conjuro & confirmo super vos Angeli fortes, sancti atque potentes, in nomine On, Hey, Heya, Ja, Je, Adonay, Saday, & in nomine Saday, qui creavit quadrupedia & anamalia reptilia, & homines in sexto die, & Adæ dedit potestatem super omnia animalia: unde benedictum sit nomen creatoris in loco suo: & per nomina Angelorum servientium in tertio exercitu, coram Agiel, Angelo magno, principe forti atque potenti: & per nomen Stellæ quæ est Venus: & per Sigillum ejus, quod quidem est sanctum: & per nomina prædicta conjuro super te Anael, qui es præpositus diei sextæ, ut pro me labores, &c.

Translation.

I conjure and confirm you, strong, holy and powerful Angels, in the name of On, Hey, Heya, Ja, Ja, Adonay, Saday; and in the name of the same Saday who, on the sixth day, created the four-footed animals, the reptiles and men and gave Adam all power over the animals: therefore blessed be the name of the Creator in his place, and by the names of the Angels who serve in the third army in the presence of Dagiel, great Angel, strong and powerful prince; and by the name of the star which is Venus, and by its seal which is holy, and by the above mentioned names, I conjure you, Anael, who is in charge of Friday which is the sixth day, to work for me, etc... (as in the Sunday conjuration).

The Spirits of the Air of Friday are subject to the West-winde; their nature is to give silver: to excite men, and incline them to luxury; to reconcile enemies through luxury; and to make marriages; to allure men to love women; to cause, or take away infirmities; and to do all things which have motion.

Common Forms of the Spirits of Venus on Friday.

They appear with a beautiful body, of medium size, with an amiable and pleasant appearance, of a white or green and sometimes golden color; their movement is similar to that of a very bright star; and for their signs, we will see near the Circle young girls frolicking and exciting the one who performs the operation to have fun with them.

Their particular forms are:

A king, a scepter in hand, mounted on a camel;

A perfectly well dressed young girl;

A young girl completely naked;

A goat;

A camel;

A dove;

A white or green outfit;

Flowers;

Savin Juniper.

CONSIDERATIONS OF SATURDAY.

The Angel of Saturday, his Seal, his Planet, and the Signe governing the Planet:

The Angels of Saturday: Cassiel, Machalan, Uriel.

The Angels of the air ruling on Saturday: Maymon, king. Abumalith, Assaibi, Balidet, ministers.

The winde which the said Angels of the air aforesaid are under: Africus (The Southwest-winde).

The perfume of Saturday: Le Sulphur.

It is already declared in the Consideration of Thursday, that there are no Angels ruling the Air, above the fifth heaven: therefore in the four Angles of the world, use those Orations which you see applied to that purpose on Thursday.

The Conjuration of Saturday.

Conjuro & confirmo super vos Caphriel vel Cassiel, Machatori, & Seraquiel Angeli fortes & potentes: & per nomen Adonay, Adonay, Adonay, Eie, Eie, Eie, Acim, Acim, Acin, Cados, Cados, Ina vel Ima, Ima, Saday, Ja, Sar, Domini formatoris seculorum, qui in septimo die quievit: & per illum qui in beneplacito suo filiis Israel in hereditatem observandum dedit, ut eum firmiter custodirent, & sanctificarent, ad habendem inde bonam in alio seculo remunerationem: & per nomina Angelorum servientium in exercitu septimo Booel Angelo magno & potenti principi: & per nomen stellæ quæ est Saturnus: & per sanctum Sigillum ejus: & per nomina prædicta conjuro super te Caphriel, qui præpositus es diei septimæ, quæ est dies Sabbati, quòd pro me labores, &c.

Translation.

I conjure and confirm upon you, Caphriel or Cassiel, laehalori and Seraqueil, strong and powerful Angels, and by the name of Adonay, Adonay, Adonay, Eie, Eie, Eie, Acim, Acim, Acim, Cados, Cados, Cados, Inavel, Ima, Ima, Saday, Ia, Sar, the Lord who formed the centuries, and who rested on the seventh day; and by Him who of His good pleasure has given to the children of Israel as an inheritance this day to be kept exactly and sanctified, to then have its reward in the next age; and by the name of the Angels who serve in the seventh army, under the guidance and command of Booel, great Angel and powerful prince; and by the name of the star which is Saturn, and by its holy seal and by the above mentioned names; I conjure upon you, Caphriel, who is in charge of Saturday which is the seventh day, that you work for me, etc. (as in the Sunday conjuration).

The Spirits of the Air of Saturday are subject to the Southwest-winde: the nature of them is to sow discordes, hatred, evil thoughts and cogitations; to give leave freely, to slay and kill every one, and to lame or maim every member. Their manner of appearing is declared in the former book.

Common Forms of the Spirits of Saturn on Saturday.

They most often appear long and slender, with a furious look, having four faces: one on the back, the other on the front of the head, these two faces having a beak; the other two faces are on their knees. They are black and transparent in color; their movement is a great agitation of winds, with an appearance of earthquakes. Their signal is to make the earth white, whiter than any snow.

Their particular forms are:
A bearded king mounted on a dragon;
A bearded old man;
An old woman leaning on a stick;
A pig;
A dragon;
An owl;
A black coat;
A scythe;
Juniper.

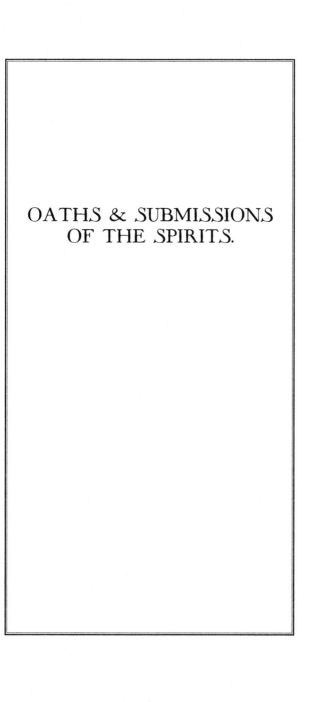

OATHS & SUBMISSIONS
OF THE SPIRITS.

Oaths & submissions
of the Spirits.

We dominant Spirits; namely, Kings, Emperors, Princes, Dukes, Counts, Marquis, Barons, Governor-Generals, Captains, Ministers, Lords & our other subjects the Spirits, acknowledge, undersign, attest, bind & swear upon the high & most sacred names of God, the Conjurations & Exorcisms contained in this Book, as also the Characters belonging to us, to be of general value & service to all those who shall make use of the present Book in all their needs & necessities whatsoever, & without exemption, according to the power we have received from God, & we ratify all the following things.

FIRSTLY.

We pledge & submit ourselves to serve faithfully all those who shall hereby request us, according to our oath, & to do or cause to be done by our subjects all desires & wills, & that no mortal shall ever have knowledge of what shall be done & executed by our ministry, & that no Spirits shall be able to give knowledge of it to anyone, though they be invoked for it. We also promise to bring them or have them bring & transport whatever is required of us, without deceit or fraud, & that everything will be good & loyal to their will, without our being able to take it back either during their life or after their death, & that we cannot expect any reward for the services we render them.

Item. We submit ourselves to appear to all those who will call us by our names contained in this present Book, in beautiful human form, without any ugliness or deformity, whenever we are called, without doing any harm to what they have received from God, nor to their five senses of nature, nor to those who will be in their company, nor to the place or houses where they will call us & this without making noise, neither lightning, nor thunder, nor lightnings, nor clatter, nor rupture, nor fracture, nor uproar, in any way whatsoever, & no living creature will be aware of our coming, that those who will call us & their companions, if they order it to us; we also oblige ourselves to answer them on all questions & requests made to us, & our answers will be true without amphibology, nor double meaning; on the contrary, we will speak good English, precisely & intelligibly; & after having satisfied what is required of us, we will withdraw in peace & without tumult, observing the same conditions in going as in coming, when they pronounce the dismissal.

Item. For the execution of all the aforesaid conditions we oblige ourselves & commit ourselves, under the penalties of the hundredfold increase of our torments, from moment to moment, & of the deprivation of our offices, honors & dignities, in witness whereof we have affixed our seals, stamps & Characters, & signed the present Book, to serve all those who will invoke us, & immediately we will do what we are ordered without any delay.

TABLES OF THE
ANGELS OF THE HOURS,
ACCORDING TO THE
COURSE OF THE DAYES.

SUNDAY ☉

HOURS OF THE DAY.		ANGELS OF THE HOURS.		HOURS OF THE NIGHT.		ANGELS OF THE HOURS.
1. Yayn	☉	Michael	1. Beron	♃	Sachiel
2. Ianor	♀	Anael	2. Barol	♂	Samael
3. Nasnia	☿	Raphael	3. Thanu	☉	Michael
4. Salla	☽	Gabriel	4. Athir	♀	Anael
5. Sadedali	♄	Cassiel	5. Mathon	☿	Raphael
6. Thamur	♃	Sachiel	6. Rana	☽	Gabriel
7. Ourer	♂	Samael	7. Netos	♄	Cassiel
8. Tanir	☉	Michael	8. Tafrac	♃	Sachiel
9. Neron	♀	Anael	9. Sassur	♂	Samael
10. Jaye	☿	Raphael	10. Aglo	☉	Michael
11. Abay	☽	Gabriel	11. Calerna	♀	Anael
12. Natalon	♄	Cassiel	12. Salam	☿	Raphael

MONDAY ☽

HOURS OF THE DAY.		ANGELS OF THE HOURS.	HOURS OF THE NIGHT.		ANGELS OF THE HOURS.
1.	Yayn	☽ Gabriel	1.	Beron	♀ Anael
2.	Ianor	♄ Cassiel	2.	Barol	☿ Raphael
3.	Nasnia	♃ Sachiel	3.	Thanu	☽ Gabriel
4.	Salla	♂ Samael	4.	Athir	♄ Cassiel
5.	Sadedali	☉ Michael	5.	Mathon	♃ Sachiel
6.	Thamur	♀ Anael	6.	Rana	♂ Samael
7.	Ourer	☿ Raphael	7.	Netos	☉ Michael
8.	Tanir	☽ Gabriel	8.	Tafrac	♀ Anael
9.	Néron	♄ Cassiel	9.	Sassur	☿ Raphael
10.	Jaye	♃ Sachiel	10.	Aglo	☽ Gabriel
11.	Abay	♂ Samael	11.	Calerna	♄ Cassiel
12.	Natalon	☉ Michael	12.	Salam	♃ Sachiel

TUESDAY ♂

HOURS OF THE DAY.		ANGELS OF THE HOURS.		HOURS OF THE NIGHT.		ANGELS OF THE HOURS.	
1.	Yayn	♂	Samael	1.	Beron	♄	Cassiel
2.	Ianor	☉	Michael	2.	Barol	♃	Sachiel
3.	Nasnia	♀	Anael	3.	Thanu	♂	Samael
4.	Salla	☿	Raphael	4.	Athir	☉	Michael
5.	Sadedali	☽	Gabriel	5.	Mathon	♀	Anael
6.	Thamur	♄	Cassiel	6.	Rana	☿	Raphael
7.	Ourer	♃	Sachiel	7.	Netos	☽	Gabriel
8.	Tanir	♂	Samael	8.	Tafrac	♄	Cassiel
9.	Néron	☉	Michael	9.	Sassur	♃	Sachiel
10.	Jaye	♀	Anael	10.	Aglo	♂	Samael
11.	Abay	☿	Raphael	11.	Calerna	☉	Michael
12.	Natalon	☽	Gabriel	12.	Salam	♀	Anael

WEDNESDAY ☿

HOURS OF THE DAY.		ANGELS OF THE HOURS.		HOURS OF THE NIGHT.		ANGELS OF THE HOURS.
1.	Yayn	☿	Raphael	1.	Beron	☉ Michael
2.	Ianor	☽	Gabriel	2.	Barol	♀ Anael
3.	Nasnia	♄	Cassiel	3.	Thanu	☿ Raphael
4.	Salla	♃	Sachiel	4.	Athir	☽ Gabriel
5.	Sadedali	♂	Samael	5.	Mathon	♄ Cassiel
6.	Thamur	☉	Michael	6.	Rana	♃ Sachiel
7.	Ourer	♀	Anael	7.	Netos	♂ Samael
8.	Tanir	☿	Raphael	8.	Tafrac	☉ Michael
9.	Néron	☽	Gabriel	9.	Sassur	♀ Anael
10.	Jaye	♄	Cassiel	10.	Aglo	☿ Raphael
11.	Abay	♃	Sachiel	11.	Calerna	☽ Gabriel
12.	Natalon	♂	Samael	12.	Salam	♄ Cassiel

THURSDSAY ♃

HOURS OF THE DAY.		ANGELS OF THE HOURS.		HOURS OF THE NIGHT.	ANGELS OF THE HOURS.	
1.	Yayn	Sachiel	♃	1. Beron	Gabriel	☽
2.	Ianor	Samael	♂	2. Barol	Cassiel	♄
3.	Nasnia	Michael	☉	3. Thanu	Sachiel	♃
4.	Salla	Anael	♀	4. Athir	Samael	♂
5.	Sadedali	Raphael	☿	5. Mathon	Michael	☉
6.	Thamur	Gabriel	☽	6. Rana	Anael	♀
7.	Ourer	Cassiel	♄	7. Netos	Raphael	☿
8.	Tanir	Sachiel	♃	8. Tafrac	Gabriel	☽
9.	Néron	Samael	♂	9. Sassur	Cassiel	♄
10.	Jaye	Michael	☉	10. Aglo	Sachiel	♃
11.	Abay	Anael	♀	11. Calerna	Samael	♂
12.	Natalon	Raphael	☿	12. Salam	Michael	☉

FRIDAY ♀

	HOURS OF THE DAY.		ANGELS OF THE HOURS.		HOURS OF THE NIGHT.		ANGELS OF THE HOURS.
1.	Yayn	♀	Anael	1.	Beron	♂	Samael
2.	Ianor	☿	Raphael	2.	Barol	☉	Michael
3.	Nasnia	☽	Gabriel	3.	Thanu	♀	Anael
4.	Salla	♄	Cassiel	4.	Athir	☿	Raphael
5.	Sadedali	♃	Sachiel	5.	Mathon	☽	Gabriel
6.	Thamur	♂	Samael	6.	Rana	♄	Cassiel
7.	Ourer	☉	Michael	7.	Netos	♃	Sachiel
8.	Tanir	♀	Anael	8.	Tafrac	♂	Samael
9.	Néron	☿	Raphael	9.	Sassur	☉	Michael
10.	Jaye	☽	Gabriel	10.	Aglo	♀	Anael
11.	Abay	♄	Cassiel	11.	Calerna	☿	Raphael
12.	Natalon	♃	Sachiel	12.	Salam	☽	Gabriel

SATURDAY ♄

HOURS OF THE DAY.		ANGELS OF THE HOURS.	HOURS OF THE NIGHT.		ANGELS OF THE HOURS.
1.	Yayn	♄ Cassiel	1.	Beron	☿ Raphael
2.	Ianor	♃ Sachiel	2.	Barol	☽ Gabriel
3.	Nasnia	♂ Samael	3.	Thanu	♄ Cassiel
4.	Salla	☉ Michael	4.	Athir	♃ Sachiel
5.	Sadedali	♀ Anael	5.	Mathon	♂ Samael
6.	Thamur	☿ Raphael	6.	Rana	☉ Michael
7.	Ourer	☽ Gabriel	7.	Netos	♀ Anael
8.	Tanir	♄ Cassiel	8.	Tafrac	☿ Raphael
9.	Néron	♃ Sachiel	9.	Sassur	☽ Gabriel
10.	Jaye	♂ Samael	10.	Aglo	♄ Cassiel
11.	Abay	☉ Michael	11.	Calerna	♃ Sachiel
12.	Natalon	♀ Anael	12.	Salam	♂ Samael

But this is to be observed by the way, that the first hour of the day, of every Country, and in every season whatsoever, is to be assigned to the Sun-rising, when he first appeareth arising in the horizon: and the first hour of the night is to be the thirteenth hour, from the first hour of the day. But of these things it is sufficiently spoken.

FINIS.

TABLE.

OATHS & SUBMISSIONS
OF THE SPIRITS

TABLES OF THE ANGELS OF THE
HOURS, ACCORDING TO THE
COURSE OF THE DAYES

Printed in Great Britain
by Amazon

42432826R00059